"Success usually comes to those who are too busy to be looking for it." …

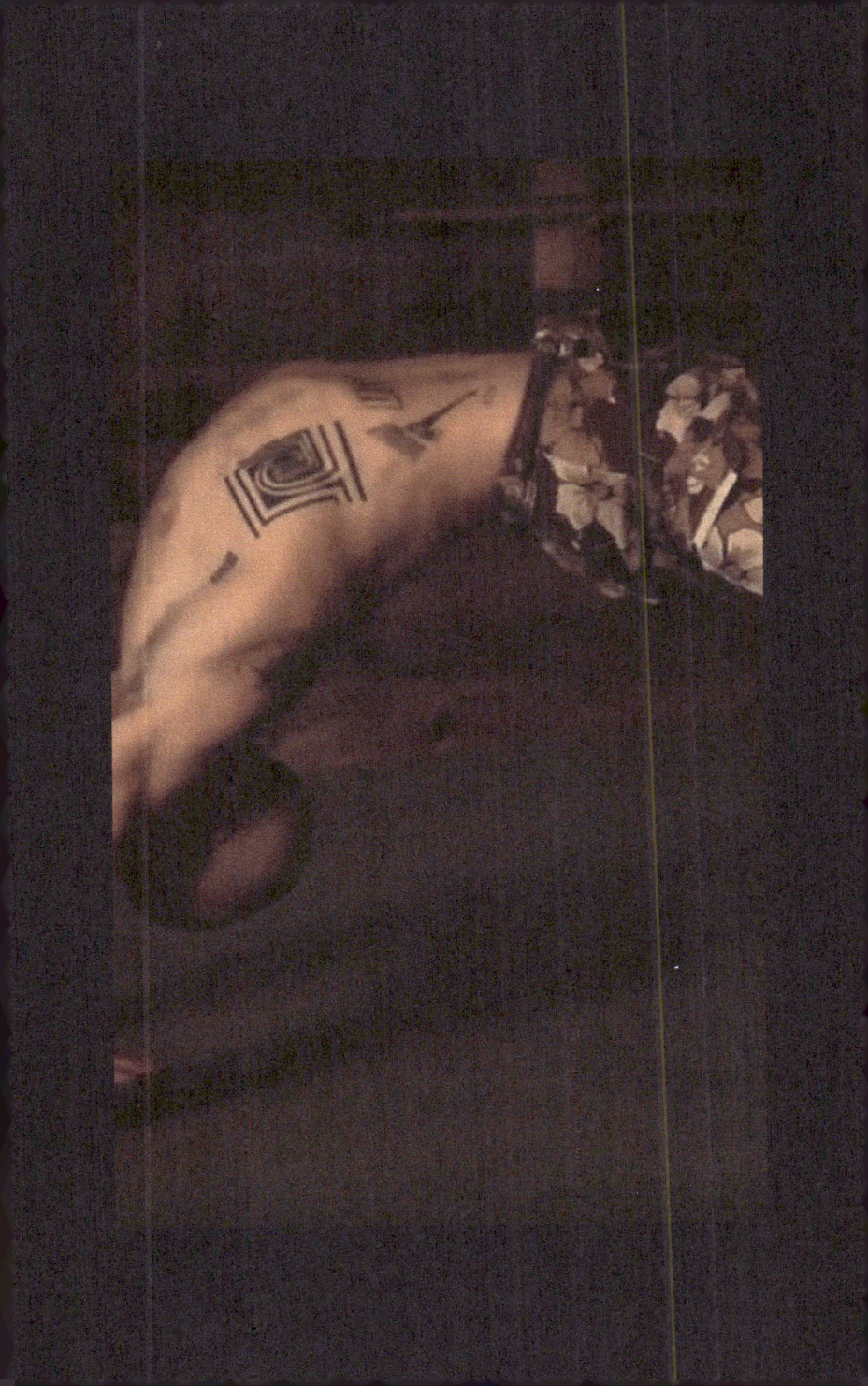

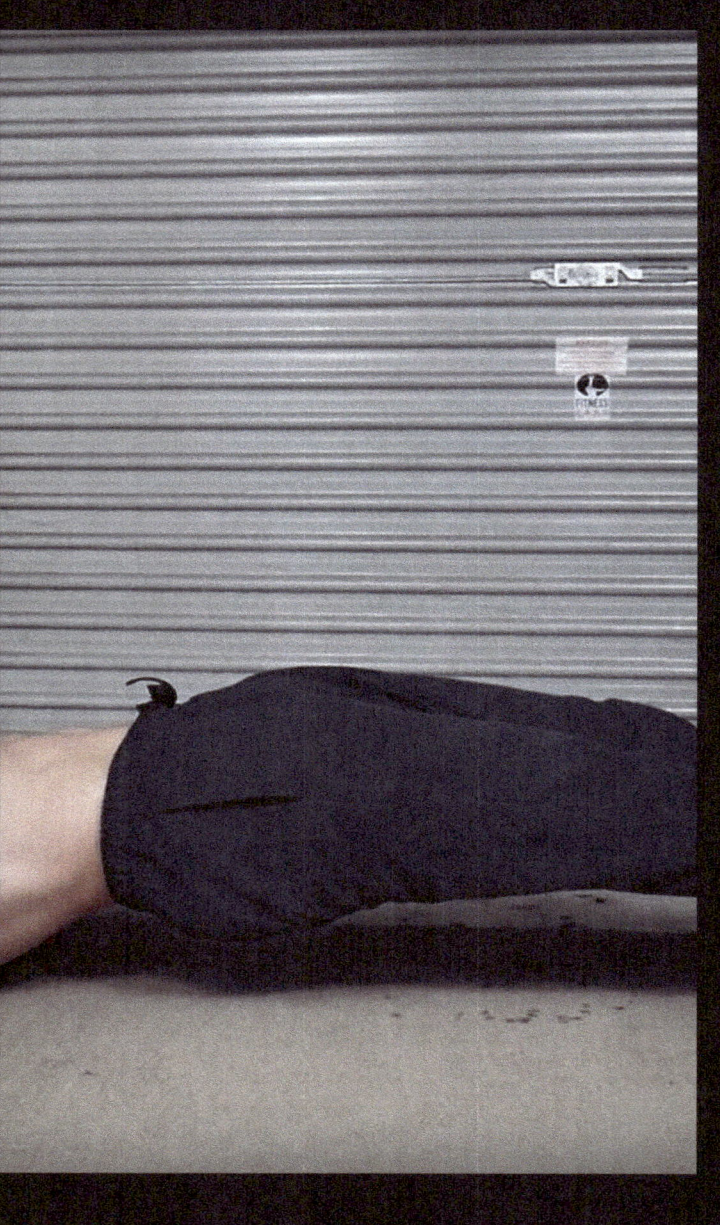

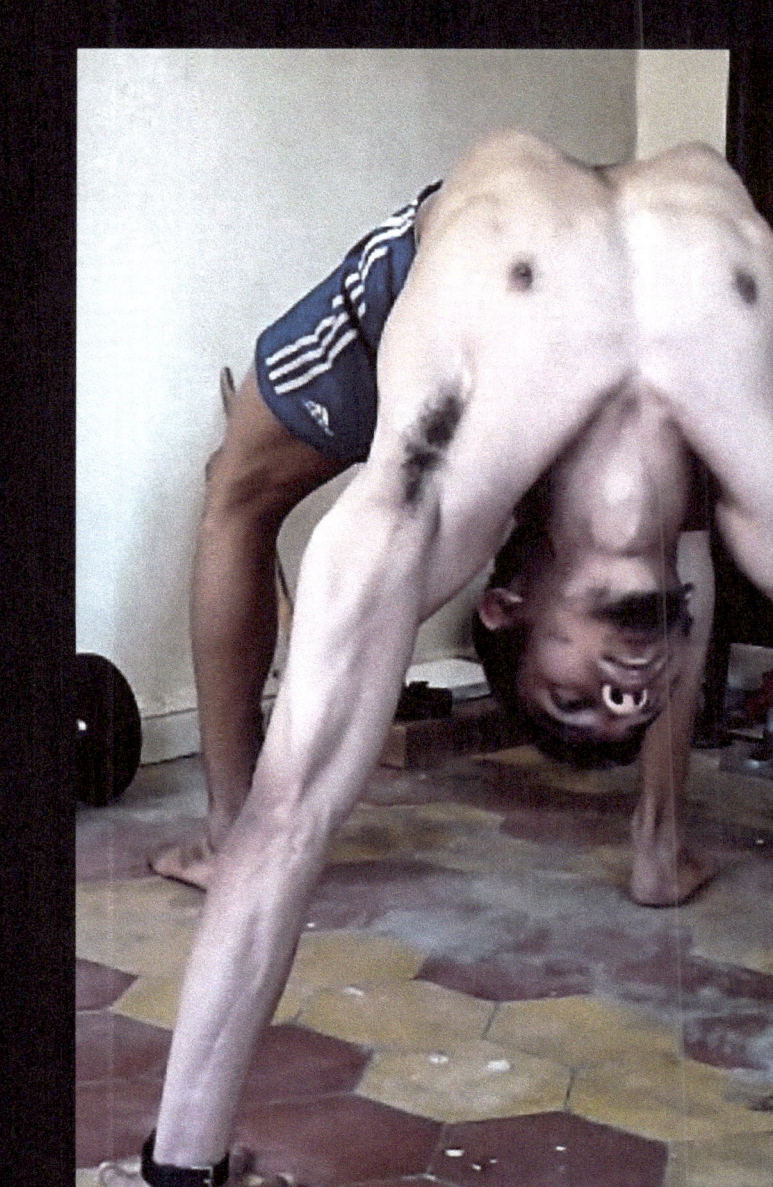

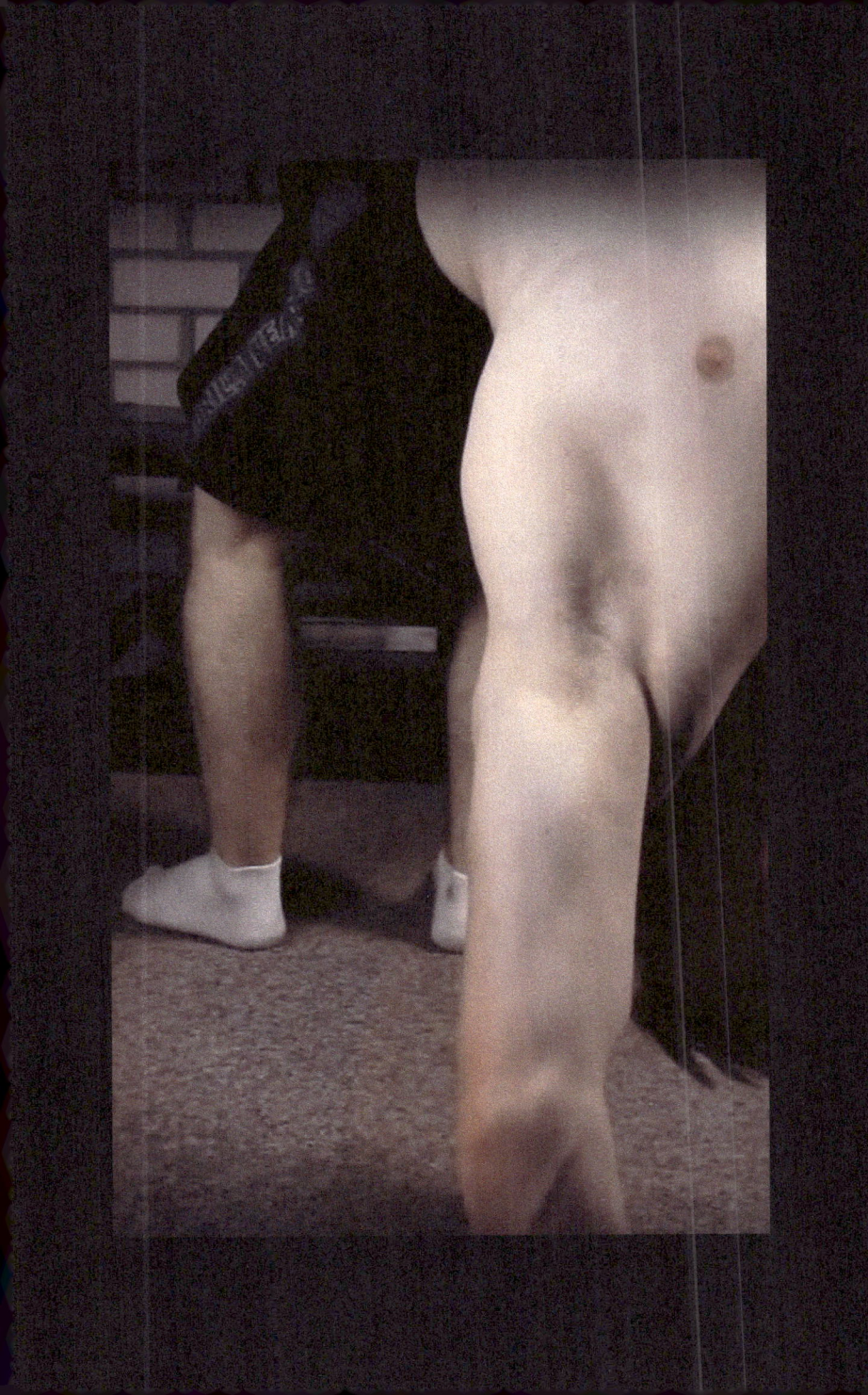

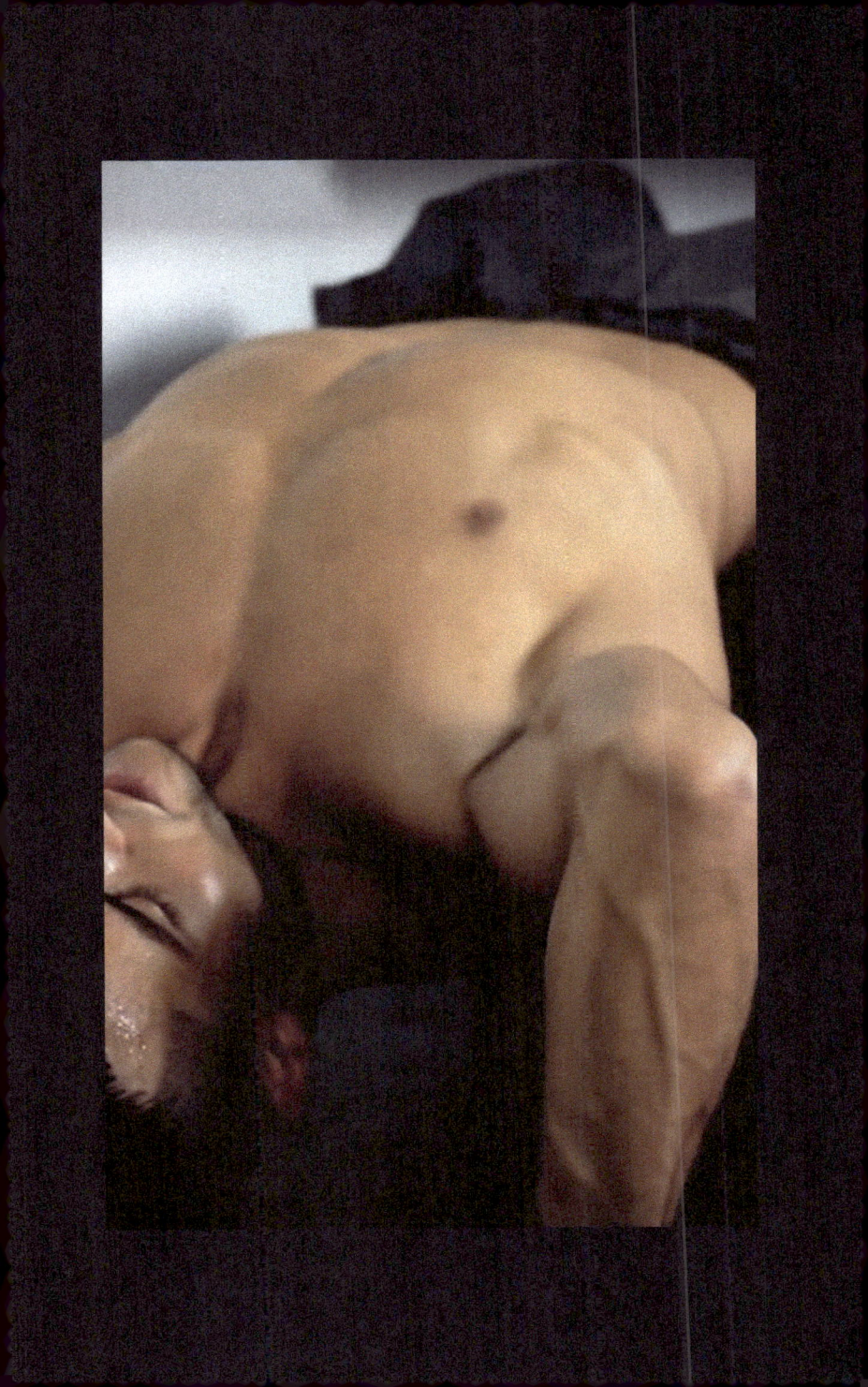

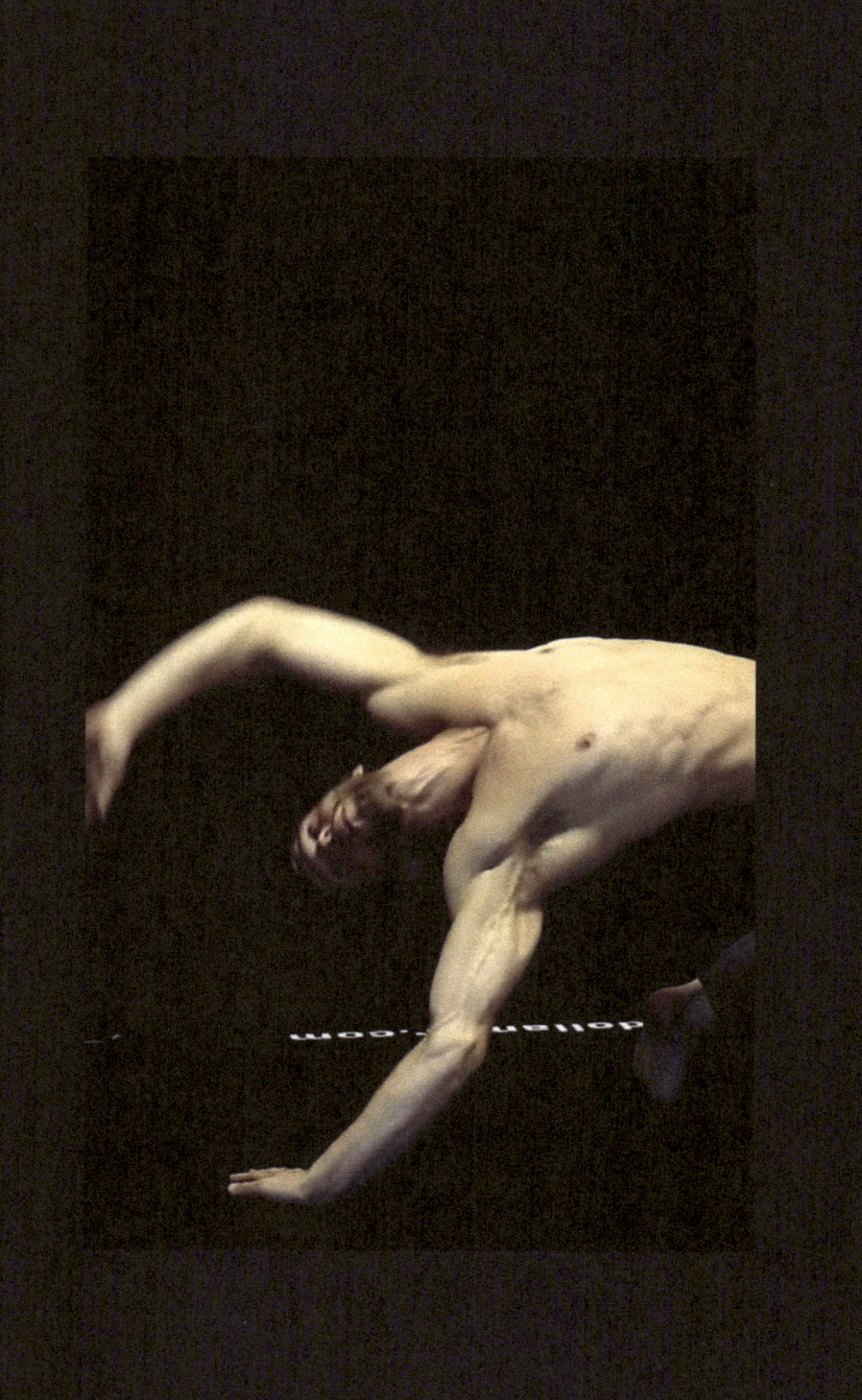

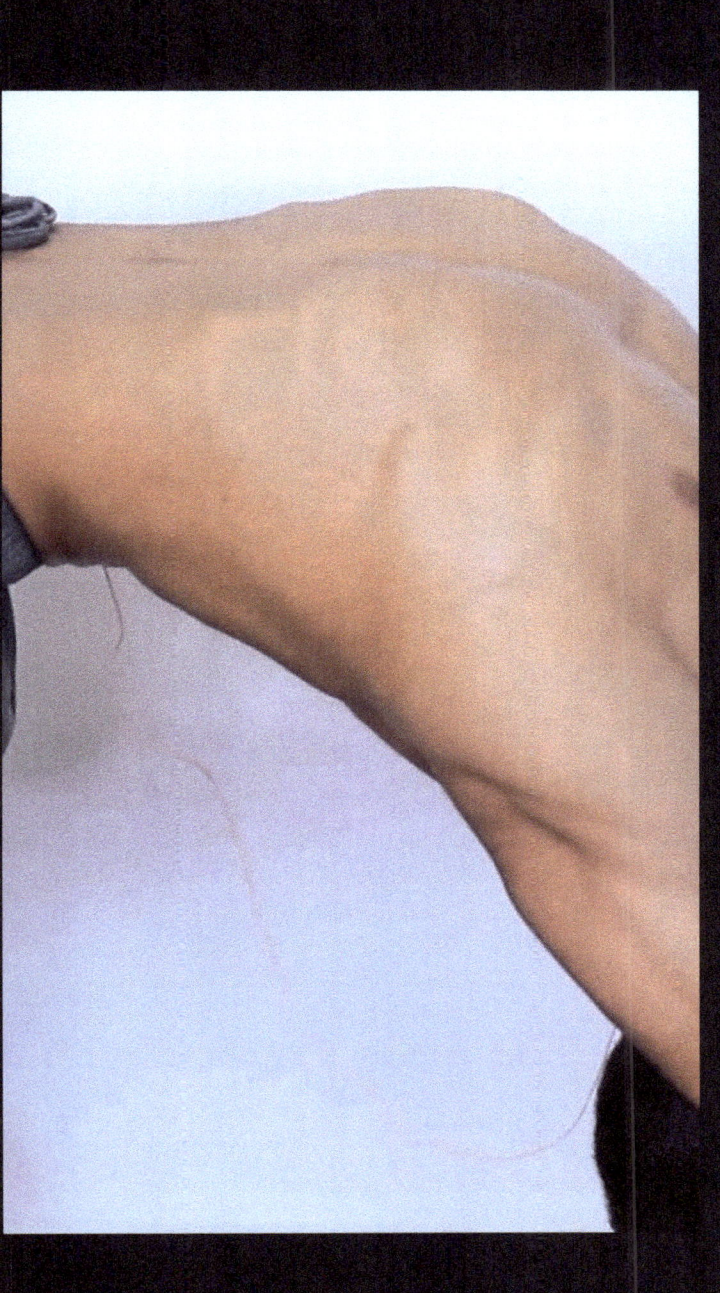

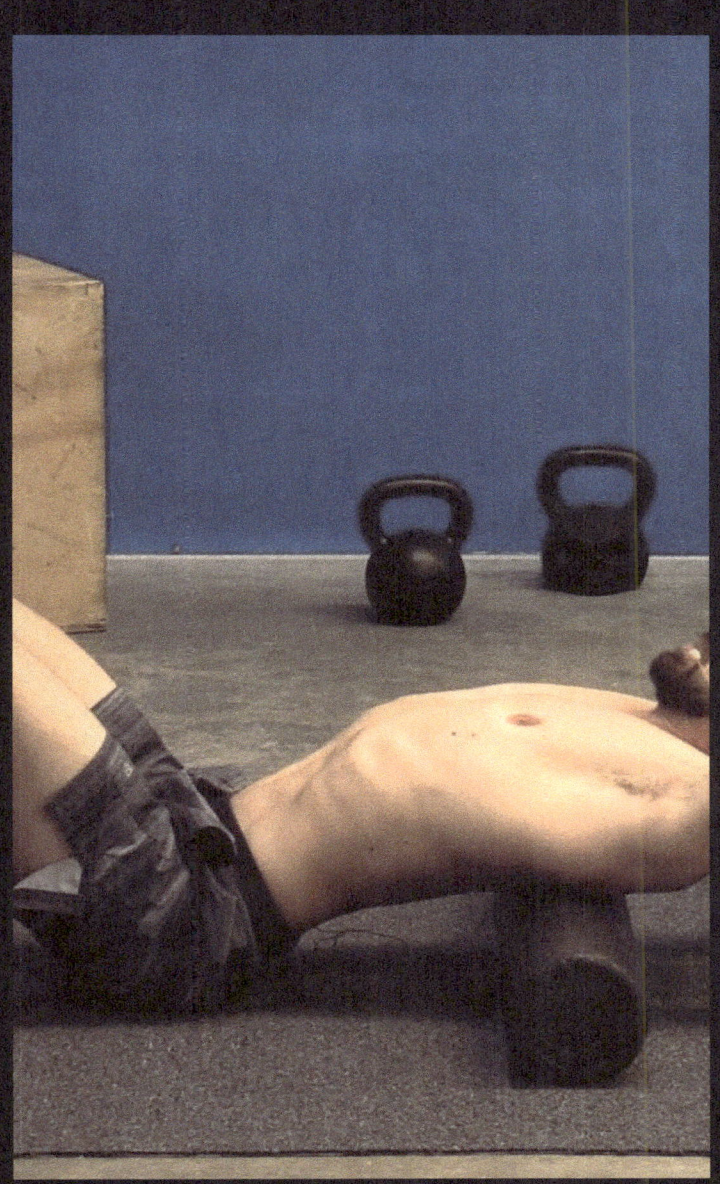

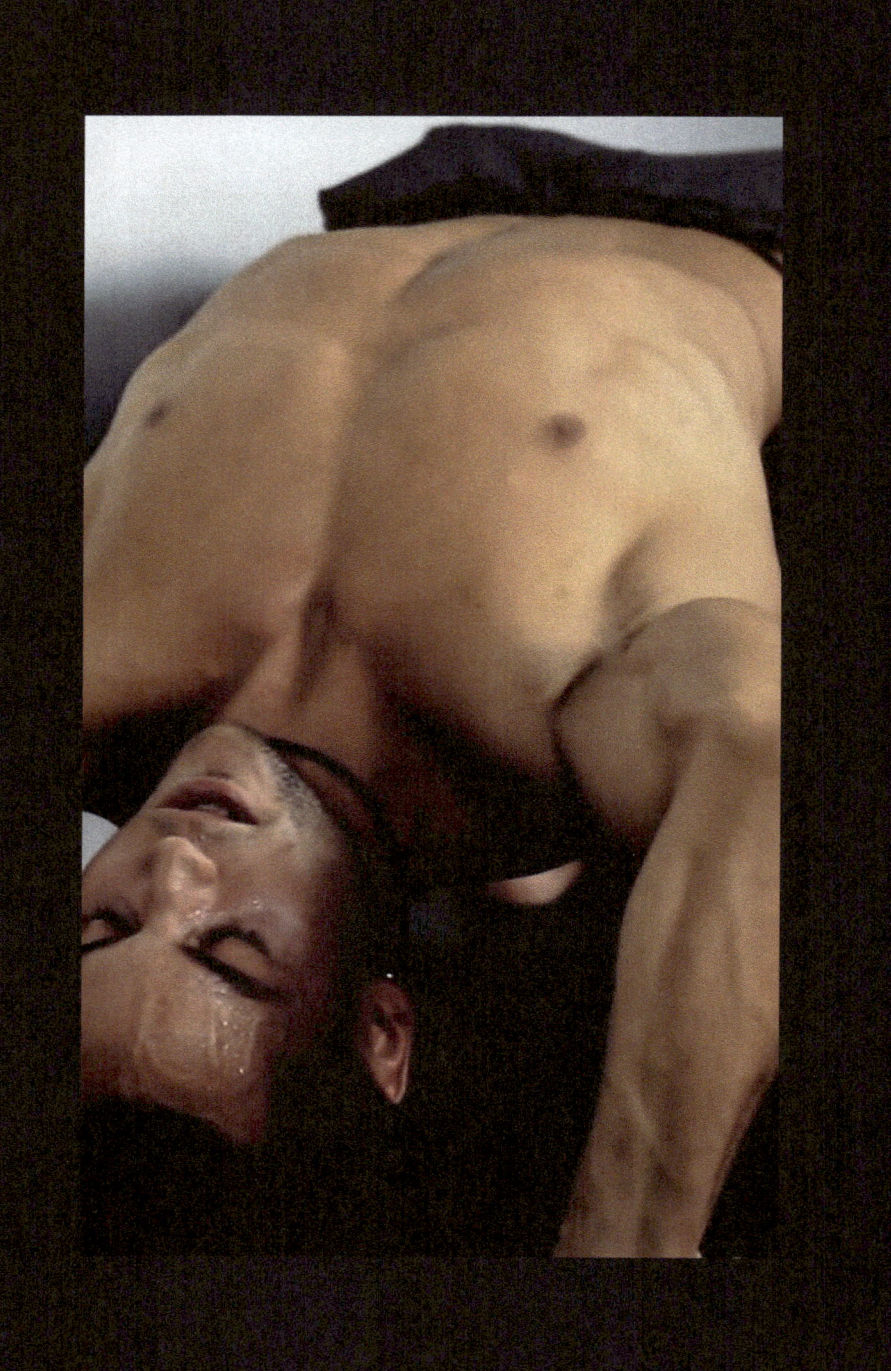

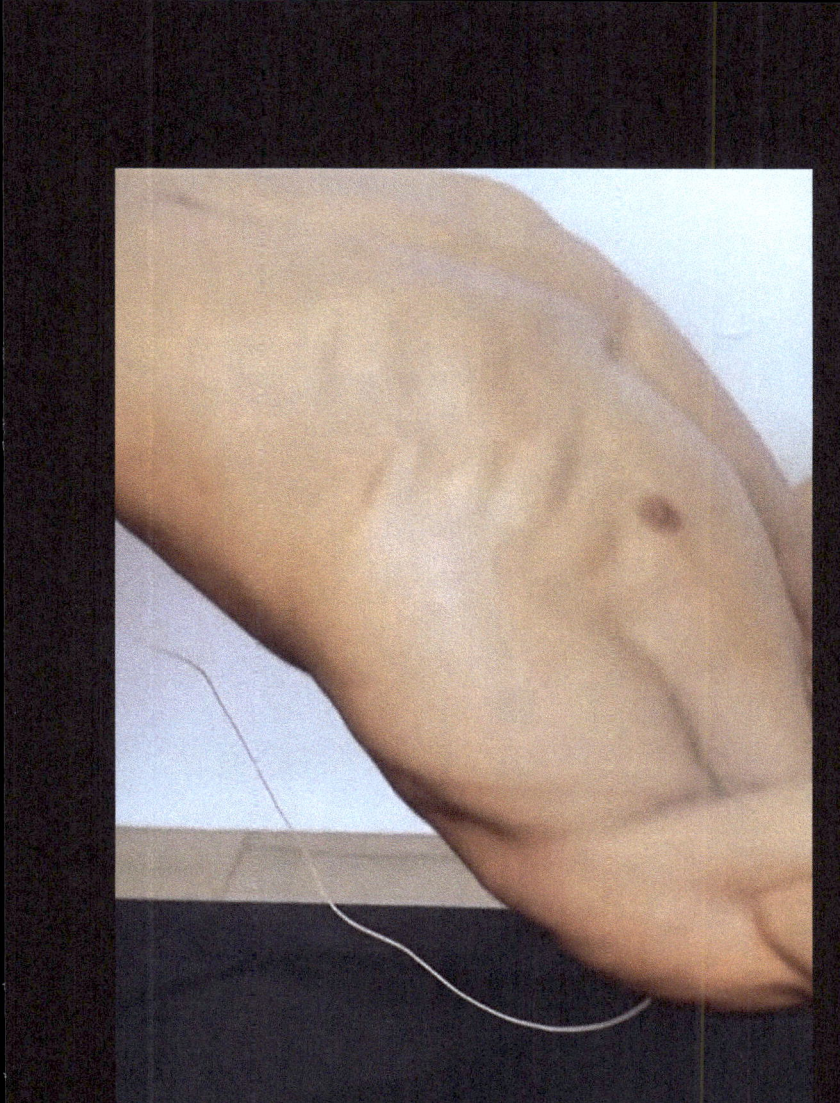

CPSIA information can be obtained
at www.ICGtesting.com
Printed in the USA
BVHW092052010519
547090BV00015B/233/P

9 780368 673641